Design: Jill Coote
Recipe Photography: Peter Barry
Recipe styling: Jacqueline Bellefontaine, Helen
Burdett, Bridgeen Deery and Wendy Devenish
Jacket and Illustration Artwork: Jane Winton,
courtesy of Bernard Thornton Artists, London
Compiled and introduced by Laura Potts
Edited by Josephine Bacon

Published by
CHARTWELL BOOKS, INC.
A Division of **BOOK SALES, INC.**
110 Enterprise Avenue
Secaucus, New Jersey 07094

CLB 3356

© 1993 CLB Publishing,

Godalming, Surrey, England

Printed and bound in Singapore

ISBN 1-55521-979-9

THE
LITTLE BOOK
· OF ·

Baking

RECIPES

An enticing selection of recipes for
mouthwatering cakes and
cookies.

CHARTWELL
BOOKS, INC.

Introduction

Walking into a kitchen and being greeted by the smell of freshly baked cake is enough to unlock a flood of childhood memories. It evokes memories of returning home from school to a house filled with tantalizing smells of baking, of eating hot biscuits in front of the fire on cold winter days, and of eating strawberry shortcake during the hot, lazy days of summer. Most importantly, people remember the sense of mystery that they felt as a child as they watched sugar and butter being creamed, as eggs were separated and beaten, and as the last of carefully weighed ingredients were incorporated into the mixture.

In days gone by, recipes were passed from generation to generation, though frequently they were not actually written down. By watching a certain cake or cookie being prepared time and time again, a child would soon learn just how much of each ingredient to add to get the perfect result, and would learn to cook from intuition and experience. To a lesser degree, the same thing happens today. Simple cakes and cookies will be the first experience that many people have of cookery. They too will have favorite recipes so familiar that they barely need to look at the method or check the measurements. Such familiarity can sometimes be limiting, with people sticking with what they know, and only rarely experimenting with new recipes and unfamiliar techniques.

The choice of recipes in this book covers a broad cross-section of the many branches of baking, and includes recipes for sponge cakes, breads and yeast cakes, as well as tarts and pastries. Some of the recipes, particularly those for cookies, are quick and easy to prepare, and act as the perfect introduction for the novice cook. Others, like the yeast breads, are more complicated and are suitable for the more experienced baker. Hopefully the recipes, which include specialties from other countries, will give you some new ideas and increase your range of skills. The step-by-step format highlights some of the techniques involved and helps you to avoid many of the most common pitfalls.

Baking can be cookery at its most creative and, with the advent of electric mixers, food processors and blenders, it no longer needs to be time-consuming. Basic techniques used in baking can now be carried out in a fraction of the time and, with the important exception of pastry, with excellent results. So it is possible for you to make delicious cakes and pastries to delight your friends and family, without necessarily spending hours in the kitchen.

Apple Tart

MAKES 1 TART

The rich pastry in this tart makes it particularly special.

PREPARATION: 30 mins
COOKING: 35-40 mins

Pastry
1½ cups all-purpose flour
Salt
3 tbsps sugar
Dash vanilla extract or 1 tsp grated lemon rind
⅔ cup butter or margarine
2 egg yolks or 1 whole egg
1-4 tbsps milk or water

Filling
1 pound dessert apples
Sugar for dredging

1. Sift the flour, salt, and sugar into a large bowl. Rub in the fat until the mixture resembles fine breadcrumbs.

Step 1 Rub the butter into the dry ingredients until the mixture resembles fine breadcrumbs.

Step 3 Press the pastry into the flan dish, making sure the base and sides are of even thickness. Trim off any excess pastry.

2. Make a well in the center and place in the egg yolks or the whole egg. Add the vanilla or lemon rind and 1 tbsp milk or water. Mix into the flour with a fork. If the pastry appears too dry, add the additional milk or water.

3. Knead together quickly until smooth. If the mixture is too soft, wrap well in plastic wrap and chill briefly.

4. Press the pastry on the base and up the sides of a flan dish and chill 15 minutes.

5. Meanwhile, prepare the fruit. Peel, core, and quarter the apples and slice thinly. Arrange the apple on the base of the flan in circles with the slices slightly overlapping. Sprinkle with sugar and bake in a preheated oven at 400°F until the pastry is pale golden-brown and the fruit is soft. Allow to cool before serving.

Royal Mazurek

SERVES 8

The pastry for this traditional Polish cake needs careful handling.

PREPARATION: 30 mins, plus 1 hr to chill the dough

COOKING: 20-30 mins

⅔ cup butter or margarine
¼ cup sugar
⅓ cup blanched almonds, finely chopped
½ tsp grated lemon rind
2½ cups all-purpose flour
Yolks of 2 hard-cooked eggs, sieved
1 raw egg yolk
Pinch salt
Pinch cinnamon
Apricot, raspberry, or cherry preserves
Confectioner's sugar

---

1. Cream the butter and the sugar together until light and fluffy. Stir in the almonds, lemon rind, flour, and egg yolks by hand. Add the raw egg yolk, a pinch of salt, and cinnamon, and mix into a smooth dough. Wrap well in plastic wrap and leave in the refrigerator for about 1 hour.

2. Roll out two-thirds of the dough and place on a greased jellyroll pan. If dough cracks,

Step 3 Arrange the strips in a latticework pattern on top of the pastry base, pressing edges together well.

press back into place. Meanwhile keep remaining dough in the refrigerator.

3. Roll out the remaining dough and cut into strips about ¼ inch thick. Arrange these strips on top of the dough in a lattice pattern and press the edges to seal.

4. Brush the pastry with a little beaten egg. Bake in a preheated 375°F oven about 20-30 minutes, or until light golden-brown and crisp. Loosen the pastry from the baking sheet but do not remove until completely cool. Place the pastry on a serving plate and spoon some preserve into each of the open spaces of the lattice work. Sprinkle lightly with confectioner's sugar before serving.

Almond Cookies

MAKES 30

When making these cookies, do not overbeat the mixture once the almonds are added, as it will become too sticky to shape.

PREPARATION: 10 mins
COOKING: 12-15 minutes per batch

½ cup butter or margarine
¼ cup superfine sugar
1 tbsp light brown sugar
1 egg, beaten
Almond extract
1 cup all-purpose flour
1 tsp baking powder
Pinch salt
2 tbsps ground almonds
2 tbsps water
30 whole blanched almonds

1. Cream the butter or margarine together with the two sugars until light and fluffy.

Step 2 Add egg and flavoring and beat until smooth.

Step 3 Shape into small balls with floured hands on a floured surface. Place well apart on cookie sheets.

2. Divide the beaten egg in half and add half to the sugar mixture with a few drops of the almond extract and beat until smooth. Reserve the remaining egg for later use. Sift the flour, baking powder, and salt into the egg mixture and add the ground almonds. Stir well by hand.

3. Shape the mixture into small balls and place well apart on a lightly-greased cookie sheet. Flatten slightly and press an almond on to the top of each one.

4. Mix the reserved egg with the water and brush each cookie before baking.

5. Place in a preheated 350°F oven and bake 12-15 minutes. Cookies will be a pale golden color when done.

Spiced Cookies

MAKES 15

Crunchy and wholesome, these spicy cookies are a delicious snack

PREPARATION: 20 mins
COOKING: 15 mins

---

1 cup wholewheat flour
½ tsp baking soda
1 tsp ground cinnamon
1 tsp ground mixed spice
¼ cup oatmeal
⅓ cup soft brown sugar
⅓ cup butter
1 tbsp dark Karo syrup
1 tbsp milk

---

1. Put the flour, baking soda, cinnamon, mixed spice, oatmeal, and sugar into a bowl and stir well.

Step 3 Pour the melted mixture into the dry ingredients and mix thoroughly to form a pliable dough.

Step 5 Flatten each ball of dough slightly with the back of a wetted spoon.

2. In a saucepan, melt the butter with the syrup and milk over a gentle heat.

3. Pour the melted mixture into the dry ingredients and beat well, until the mixture forms a pliable dough.

4. Divide the mixture into about 15 small balls. Place these onto lightly-greased cookie sheets, keeping them well spaced, to allow the mixture to spread.

5. Flatten each ball with the back of a wetted spoon, and bake in a preheated 350°F oven for 15 minutes, or until golden-brown.

6. Allow the cookies to cool on the baking sheet before removing them.

Strawberry Shortcakes

SERVES 6

The base for delicious miniature shortcakes can be made in advance.

PREPARATION: 30-35 mins
COOKING: 15 mins

2 cups all-purpose flour
1 tbsp baking powder
Pinch salt
2 tbsps sugar
⅔ cup cream cheese, softened
3 tbsps butter or margarine
1 egg, beaten
¾ fl oz milk
Melted butter
1 pound fresh or frozen strawberries
Juice of half an orange
1¼ cups whipped cream

1. Sift the flour, baking powder, salt, and sugar into a large bowl.

2. Combine with the cheese and butter or margarine.

3. Blend in the egg and enough milk to make a firm dough.

4. Knead lightly on a floured surface and then roll out to a thickness of ½ inch.

5. Cut the dough into an even number of

Step 5 Brush one half of the dough circles with butter and place the remaining halves on top, pressing down lightly.

circles. Re-roll the trimmings and cut as before. Brush half of the circles with the melted butter and place the other halves on top, pressing down lightly. Bake on an ungreased cookie sheet about 15 minutes in a pre-heated 425°F oven. Allow to cool slightly and then transfer to a wire rack.

6. Hull the strawberries and wash well. Purée half of them with the orange juice. Cut the remaining strawberries in half and combine with the paste.

7. Separate the shortcakes in half and place the bottom halves on serving plates. Spoon over the strawberry sauce and the cream.

8. Place the tops of the shortcake on top of the cream.

Carrot Cake

MAKES 1 LOAF

Carrots have long been used as a sweet ingredient, and this cake is moist and absolutely delicious.

PREPARATION: 30 mins
COOKING: 45-50 mins

¾ cup butter
¾ cup soft brown sugar
2 eggs, beaten
2 cups all-purpose flour
1½ tsps baking soda
½ tsp baking powder
½ tsp ground cinnamon
¼ tsp cardamom seeds, crushed
2 cups peeled grated carrots
⅓ cup raisins
¼ cup walnuts, chopped
2 tbsps clear honey
Confectioner's sugar, for dredging

1. Cream the butter and sugar together, until they are light and fluffy.

Step 1 Cream the margarine and sugar together, until they are light and fluffy.

Step 3 Fold the dry ingredients carefully, but thoroughly, into the egg mixture, using a metal spoon.

2. Add the eggs, a little at a time, beating well after each addition.

3. Mix the flour with the baking soda, baking powder, cinnamon, and cardamom and fold into the egg mixture.

4. Stir in the carrots, raisins, and nuts, along with the honey. Mix well, to blend thoroughly.

5. Pour the mixture into a well-buttered 10-inch loaf pan. Bake in a preheated 350°F oven for 45-50 minutes, or until a fine metal skewer comes out clean when inserted into the center of the cake.

6. Cool the cake in the pan for 10-15 minutes, before turning out carefully onto a wire rack to cool completely.

7. Dredge the cake with confectioner's sugar before serving.

Spiced Cranberry Nut Coffee Bread

MAKES 1 LOAF

Coffee breads don't rely on yeast to make them rise so they are quick and easy to prepare.

PREPARATION: 25 mins
COOKING: 1 hr

---

2 cups all-purpose flour
1 tsp baking powder
1 cup sugar
1 tsp baking soda
Pinch salt
¼ tsp ground nutmeg
¼ tsp ground ginger
½ cup orange juice
2 tbsps butter, melted
4 tbsps water
1 egg, beaten
½ cup fresh cranberries, roughly chopped
½ cup hazelnuts, roughly chopped
confectioner's sugar

Step 1 Pour in the liquid ingredients and gradually incorporate the flour from the outside edge.

1. Sift the dry ingredients and spices into a large mixing bowl. Pour in the orange juice, melted butter, water, and egg and beat the mixture with a wooden spoon.

2. Add the cranberries and nuts and stir to mix.

3. Lightly grease a loaf pan about 9 × 5 inches. Press a strip of parchment paper on the base and up the sides. Lightly grease the paper and flour the whole inside of the pan. Spoon in the bread mixture and bake in a pre-heated 325°F oven about 1 hour, or until a skewer inserted into the center of the loaf comes out clean.

4. Remove from the pan, carefully peel off the paper and cool on a wire rack. Lightly dust with confectioner's sugar and cut into slices to serve.

Gingerbread

MAKES ONE

Molasses and fresh ginger combine to make this favorite family cake.

PREPARATION: 15 mins
COOKING: 1-1½ hrs

½ cup butter
½ cup black strap molasses
1 cup light soft brown sugar
¼ cup hot water
2½ cups all-purpose flour
2 tsps baking powder
2 tsps fresh ginger root, peeled and grated
1 tsp grated nutmeg
1 egg, beaten

1. Put the butter, molasses, and sugar into a large saucepan. Heat gently, stirring all the time, until the sugar and butter have melted together.

Step 1 Melt the butter, molasses, and sugar together in a large saucepan.

Step 6 The cake is done when a skewer inserted into the center comes out clean.

2. Pour in the hot water, mix well and set aside.

3. Sift the flour and baking powder into a large bowl. Add the ginger, nutmeg, and beaten egg.

4. Gradually beat in the molasses mixture, using a wooden spoon and drawing the flour from the outside into the center.

5. Line the base of a 7-inch square cake pan with lightly-greased parchment paper.

6. Pour the gingerbread mixture into the cake tin, and bake in a preheated oven 325°F 1-1½ hours, testing during this time with a skewer which should come out clean when the cake is cooked.

7. Allow the cake to cool in the pan, before turning out onto a wire rack.

Poppyseed Cake

MAKES 2 ROLLS

A version of an ever-popular Polish Christmas cake.

PREPARATION: 1 hr
COOKING: 45-50 mins

Pastry Dough
6 cups all-purpose flour
¾ cup sugar
¾ cup butter or margarine
2 eggs
3-4 fl oz milk
2 tbsps fresh yeast or 1 package dried yeast

Filling
1 cup poppyseeds, ground in a coffee grinder
1¾ cups milk
⅓ cup butter or margarine
⅔ cup honey
¼ cup ground walnuts
⅓ cup raisins
1 tbsp finely chopped candied peel
2 eggs
½ cup sugar
⅓ cup brandy
1 egg, beaten with 2 tsp water

1. To make the dough, cream the butter and sugar, then gradually add the eggs, beating between each addition. Heat the milk until lukewarm, dissolve the yeast in it, and add to the other ingredients. Sift in the flour and a pinch of salt and knead well.

2. Knead the dough on a lightly-floured

Step 5 Roll up the dough as for a jellyroll.

surface, stretching it well. When the dough springs back fairly quickly to the touch, place it in a lightly-greased bowl, cover and leave for 1 hour in a warm place to rise.

3. Boil milk for filling and add poppyseeds. Cook gently 30 minutes, stirring often, until the mixture forms a thick paste.

4. Melt the butter and add honey, walnuts, raisins and peel. Add the poppyseeds and cook gently 15 minutes, stirring well. Beat the eggs and sugar, then combine with the poppyseed mixture. Cook slowly, stirring constantly to thicken. Add the brandy then set aside.

5. When the dough has doubled in bulk, knock it back and knead for a few minutes. Divide dough in half. Roll each half out thinly on a floured surface. Spread the filling evenly over each piece, roll up as for a jellyroll and press the ends together. Place on a greased cookie sheet. Brush with beaten egg mixture. Bake in a preheated 375°F oven 45-50 minutes.

Saffron Babas

MAKES 2 CAKES
A light textured yeast cake.

PREPARATION: 2 hrs
COOKING: 1 hr

2½ cups all-purpose flour
1¾ cups lukewarm milk
1 cake fresh yeast or 1 envelope dried yeast
¾ cup sugar
8 egg yolks
4 egg whites
Grated rind of 1 lemon
3 tbsps brandy
Pinch saffron powder
8 cups all-purpose flour
Pinch salt
¾ cup melted butter, slightly cooled
½ cup yellow raisins
1 tbsp chopped candied peel

1. Sift 1½ cups flour into a large mixing bowl. Combine the milk and yeast and pour into the flour. Mix well with a wooden spoon.

2. Cover the batter and leave in a warm place for 1 hour, until it doubles in bulk and the top becomes bubbly.

3. Combine the sugar together with the egg yolks, egg whites, lemon rind, brandy, and saffron. Mix with the yeast mixture and add the

Step 2 Leave in a warm place until doubled in bulk and bubbly on top.

remaining flour and salt. Knead the dough by hand about 30 minutes on a well-floured surface.

4. Place the dough back in the bowl and add the butter, raisins, and peel. Knead until it is smooth and elastic. Divide in 2 equal portions. Butter 2 × 10-inch round cake pans very thickly and place in the dough, patting out evenly. Cover and put in a warm place to rise until it fills the pan. Bake in a pre-heated 400°F oven about 1 hour.

5. Test with a metal skewer. If the skewer comes out clean when inserted into the center of the babas the cakes are done. Leave to cool in the pans about 10-14 minutes and then remove to a cooling rack. Sprinkle with sugar or drizzle with thin frosting.

Chocolate Cinnamon Bread

MAKES 1 LOAF

Pull this bread apart to serve in individual pieces rather than slicing it.

PREPARATION: 2 hrs
COOKING: 45-50 mins

Dough
4 tbsps warm water
1 tsp sugar
1 envelope dry yeast
3-3½ cups all-purpose flour
3 tbsps sugar
Pinch salt
6 tbsps butter, softened
5 eggs, beaten

Topping
½ cup butter, melted
1 cup sugar
2 tsps cinnamon
2 tsps cocoa
¾ cup finely chopped nuts

1. Sprinkle 1 tbsp sugar and the yeast on top of the water and leave it in a warm place until foaming.

2. Sift 3 cups of flour into a bowl and add the sugar and salt. Rub in the butter until completely blended.

3. Add 2 eggs and the yeast mixture, mixing in well. Add the remaining eggs, one at a time, until the mixture forms a soft, spongy dough.

Step 5 Roll the dough in melted butter and then in the sugar mixture.

Add remaining flour as necessary. Knead for 10 minutes on a lightly-floured surface until smooth.

4. Place the dough in a greased bowl, cover loosely, and put in a warm place. Leave to stand for 1-1½ hours or until doubled in bulk.

5. Butter a ring mold liberally. Knock the dough down and knead it again for about 5 minutes. Shape into balls about 2 inches in diameter. Mix the topping ingredients together except for the melted butter. Roll the dough balls in the butter and then in the sugar mixture.

6. Place the dough balls in the bottom of the mold. Cover and allow to rise again about 15 minutes. Bake in a pre-heated 350°F oven for about 45-50 minutes. Loosen from the pan and turn out while still warm.

Lemon and Raisin Coffee Cakes

MAKES ABOUT 24

*Cooked rice is the surprise ingredient in these cakes that are crisp outside,
yet soft and light inside.*

PREPARATION: 40 mins
COOKING: 40-45 mins

½ cup long-grain rice
1 cup all-purpose flour
1 tsp baking powder
Pinch salt
½ cup sugar
2 eggs, separated
6 tbsps milk
Grated rind of 1 lemon
¼ cup raisins

1. Cook the rice, rinse, drain and leave to cool.

2. Sift the flour, baking powder, and salt into a mixing bowl and stir in the sugar.

3. Beat the egg yolks with the milk and add

Step 4 Mix a spoonful of egg white into the rice mixture to lighten it. Fold in the remaining whites using a large spoon.

Step 5 Drop the mixture by spoonfuls on a hot griddle or in a skillet. Cook until brown on both sides.

gradually to the dry ingredients, stirring constantly, to make a thick batter. Stir in the rice.

4. Beat the egg whites until stiff but not dry and fold into the batter along with the lemon rind and raisins.

5. Lightly oil a heavy skillet and place over moderate heat. When the pan is hot, drop in about 1 tbsp of batter and if necessary, spread into a small circle with the back of the spoon.

6. Cook until the mixture is brown on one side and bubbles form on the top. Turn over and cook the other side. Cook 4-6 at a time.

7. Repeat until all the batter is used, keeping the cakes warm. Serve plain or buttered.

Cornmeal Muffins

MAKES 12

These muffins are slightly sweet and crumbly.

PREPARATION: 20 mins
COOKING: 14 mins

---

1 cup all-purpose flour
2 tbsps sugar
2 tsps baking powder
½ tsp salt
¾ cup yellow cornmeal
1 egg, beaten
4 tbsps oil
1⅓ cups milk

---

1. Pre-heat the oven to 450°F. Grease a 12-cup muffin pan liberally with oil. Heat the pan 5 minutes in the oven.

Step 2 Sift the dry ingredients into a large bowl, leaving a well in the center.

Step 5 Spoon the batter into the prepared pans. It may be slightly lumpy.

2. Sift the flour, sugar, baking powder, and salt into a large bowl. Add the cornmeal and stir to blend, leaving a well in the center.

3. Combine the egg, oil, and milk and pour into the well.

4. Beat with a wooden spoon, gradually incorporating the dry ingredients into the liquid. Do not overbeat the mixture. It may be slightly lumpy.

5. Spoon the batter into the pan and bake about 14 minutes.

6. Cool briefly in the pan and then remove to a wire rack to cool further. Serve warm.

Pecan Pastries

MAKES 12

These sweet, nutty pastries are deep-fried to make them light and crisp.

PREPARATION: 30 mins
COOKING: 2 mins

1 cup all-purpose flour
1 tsp baking powder
¼ tsp salt
4 tbsps cold water
Oil for frying
2 cups dark corn syrup
⅓ cup finely chopped pecans

1. Sift the flour, baking powder, and salt together in a large bowl. Make a well in the center and pour in the cold water.

Step 1 Sift the dry ingredients into a bowl and make a well in the center.

Step 3 On a floured surface, roll out each piece until very thin.

2. Mix until a stiff dough forms, and then knead by hand until smooth.

3. Divide the dough into 12 portions, each about the size of a walnut. Roll out each portion of dough on a floured surface until very thin.

4. Heat the oil in a deep fat fryer to 350°F. Drop each piece of dough into the hot fat using two forks. Twist the dough just as it hits the oil. Cook one at a time until light brown.

5. In a large saucepan, boil the syrup until it forms a soft ball when dropped into cold water.

6. Drain the pastries on paper towels after frying and dip carefully into the hot syrup. Sprinkle with pecans before the syrup sets and allow to cool before serving.

Flourless Chocolate Cake

SERVES 6

This soufflé cake is adored by chocolate lovers everywhere.

PREPARATION: 15 minutes
COOKING: 1 hr 15 mins

---

1 pound plain chocolate
2 tbsps strong coffee
2 tbsps brandy
6 eggs
3 tbsps sugar
1¼ cups whipping cream
Confectioner's sugar
Fresh whole strawberries

---

1. Melt the chocolate in the top of a double boiler or in a microwave oven. Stir in the coffee and brandy and leave to cool slightly.

2. Beat the eggs lightly and then, using an electric mixer, gradually beat in the sugar until the mixture is thick. When the beaters are lifted the mixture should mound slightly.

3. Whip the cream until soft peaks form.

4. Beat the chocolate, and gradually add the egg mixture to it.

5. Fold in the cream and pour the cake mixture into a well-greased deep 9-inch cake pan with a disk of parchment paper in the bottom. Bake

Step 5 Pour the cake mixture into the prepared pan and then place it in a water bath.

in a pre-heated 350°F oven in a bain marie. To make a bain marie, use a roasting pan and fill with warm water to come halfway up the side of the cake pan.

6. Bake about 1 hour and then turn off the oven, leaving the cake inside to stand for 15 minutes. Loosen the sides of the cake carefully from the pan and allow the cake to cool completely before unmolding.

7. Invert the cake onto a serving platter and carefully peel off the paper. Place strips of parchment paper on top of the cake, leaving even spaces in between the strips. Sprinkle the top with confectioner's sugar and carefully lift off the paper strips. Decorate with whole strawberries.

Almond Torte

MAKES 1 CAKE
Whipped egg whites make this cake light and fluffy.

PREPARATION: 30 mins
COOKING: 30-40 mins

½ cup dry breadcrumbs
½ cup milk
1 tbsp rum
6 tbsps butter or margarine
3 tbsps sugar
6 eggs, separated
6 tbsps ground roasted almonds
2 cups heavy cream
1 tbsp sugar
1 tbsp rum
2 tbsps roasted almonds, finely chopped
Whole blanched almonds, toasted

1. Preheat the oven to 350°F. Soak the breadcrumbs in milk and rum in a large bowl.

Step 2 Fold the egg whites into the crumb mixture along with the almonds, using a large spoon or a rubber spatula.

Step 4 Sandwich the layers of cake together with the almond cream.

2. In a separate bowl, cream the butter and sugar until light and fluffy. Beat in the egg yolks, one at a time, and then add to the crumb mixture. Beat the egg whites until stiff and fold into the crumb mixture along with the almonds.

3. Grease and flour three 8-inch round cake pans. Divide the cake mixture among the pans and bake 30-40 minutes. Allow to cool briefly in the pans, loosen the sides and remove the cakes to a rack to finish cooling.

4. Whip the cream and the sugar with the rum. Reserve one third of the cream for the top and fold the finely chopped almonds into the remaining two thirds. Sandwich the cake layers together with the almond cream and spread a layer of plain cream on top, reserving some for piping.

5. Pipe out rosettes with the remaining cream on top of the cake. Decorate with the whole almonds.

Cinnamon Buttercream Cake

MAKES 1 CAKE

A cake that doesn't need baking is convenient any time, and perfect for summer.

PREPARATION: 45 mins

1¼ cups sugar
1 cinnamon stick
6 tbsps water
8 egg yolks
2 cups unsalted butter, softened
24 boudoir or lady finger cookies
6 tbsps brandy
3 tbsps toasted almonds, roughly chopped
3 squares plain chocolate, coarsely grated

1. Put the sugar, water, and cinnamon stick in a small, heavy-based saucepan and bring to the boil, stirring until the sugar dissolves.

2. Allow to boil briskly without stirring until the syrup reaches a temperature of 236°F on a candy thermometer.

3. While the sugar syrup is boiling, beat the egg yolks in a large bowl until they are thick. Soften the butter until light and fluffy.

4. When the syrup is ready, quickly pour it in a thin, steady stream into the egg yolks, beating constantly.

5. Continue beating until the mixture is thick and creamy. Allow to cool.

6. Beat in the softened butter, a spoonful at a time. Chill the mixture until it is of spreading consistency.

Step 4 Pour the prepared syrup in a thin, steady stream onto the egg yolks while beating with an electric whisk.

7. Cut the finger cookies to fit closely together in a 8-inch square cake pan. Line the pan with lightly-greased aluminum foil or nonstick baking paper.

8. Spread some of the buttercream lightly on one side of the cookies and place them, frosting side down, in the pan. Cut small pieces of cookies to fill in any corners, if necessary.

9. Sprinkle with half of the brandy. Spread over another layer of buttercream and place on the remaining cookies. Sprinkle over the remaining brandy and cover the top with buttercream, reserving some for the sides. Place the cake in the refrigerator and chill until firm.

10. When the frosting is firm, remove the cake from the refrigerator and lift it out of the pan, using the foil or paper. Slide onto a flat surface and spread the sides with the remaining buttercream. Press the almonds into the sides and decorate the top with grated chocolate.

Guinness Cake

MAKES 1 CAKE

This dark, moist fruit cake makes an ideal Christmas, or rich birthday cake.

PREPARATION: 20 mins
COOKING: 2 hrs

1 cup margarine
¾ cup soft brown sugar
1¼ cups Guinness or stout
1 cup raisins
1 cup currants
1 cup yellow raisins
½ cup chopped mixed peel
5 cups wholewheat flour
1 tsp mixed spice
1 tsp nutmeg
½ tsp baking soda
3 eggs, beaten

1. Grease and line a 9-inch cake pan with nonstick baking paper.

2. Put the margarine, sugar, and Guinness into

Step 1 Line the base and the sides of the greased cake pan with parchment or baking paper, making sure that it fits well.

Step 3 Simmer the dried fruits and peel in the sugar and Guinness mixture for 5 minutes.

a large saucepan and bring the ingredients slowly to the boil, stirring all the time, until the sugar and the margarine have melted.

3. Stir the dried fruits and peel into the Guinness mixture, and bring all the ingredients back to the boil. Simmer 5 minutes. Remove from the heat and leave until the mixture is quite cold.

4. Put the flour, spices, and baking soda into a large mixing bowl.

5. Beat the cooled fruit mixture and the eggs into the flour, mixing well with a wooden spoon, to ensure that the flour is thoroughly incorporated and there are no lumps.

6. Pour the cake mixture into the prepared pan, and bake in the center of a preheated 325°F oven, 2 hours.

7. Cool the cake in the pan, before turning it out.

Index

Pecan Pastries are both sweet and nutty.